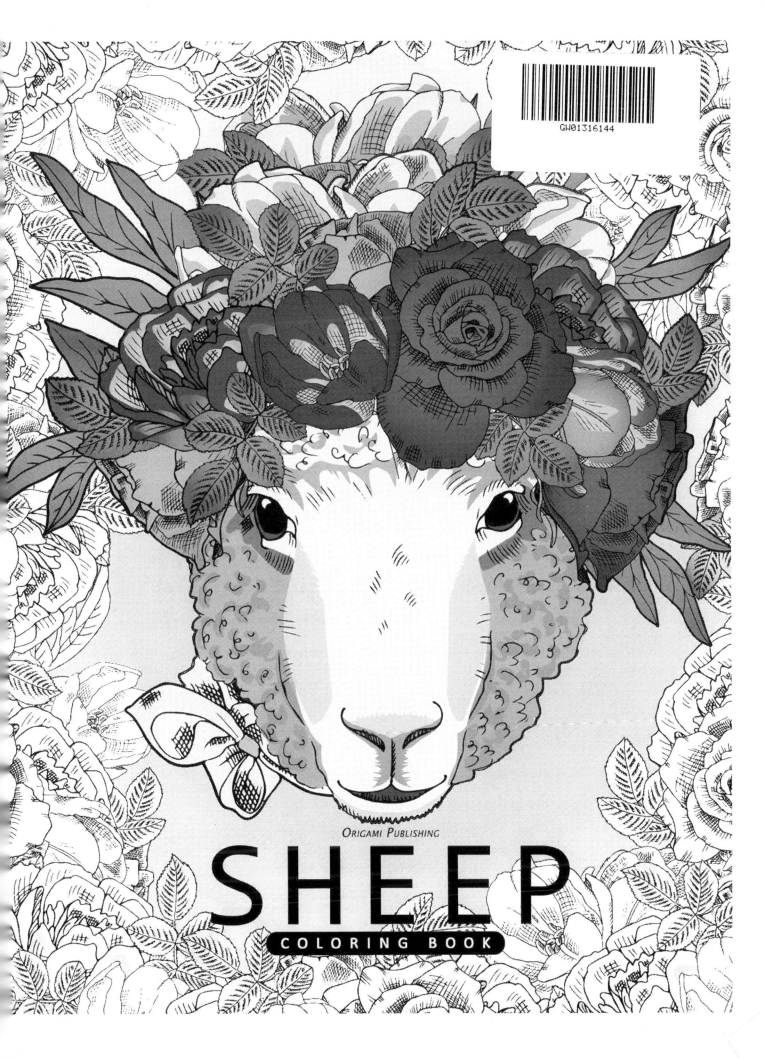

PUBLISHED IN 2018 BY
ORIGAMI PUBLISHING

COPYRIGHT 'ILLUSTRATIONS' 2018 ORIGAMI PUBLISHING
ALL RIGHT RESERVED.'NO PART OF THIS PUBLICATION MAY BE REPRODUCED OR TRANSMITTED IN ANY
FORM OR BY ANY MEANS, ELECTRONIC OR MECHANICAL, INCLUDING PHOTOCOPY RECORDING OR ANY
INFORMATION STORAGE SYSTEM AND RETRIEVAL SYSTEM WITHOUT PERMISSION IN WRITING
BY ORIGAMI PUBLISHING

PRINTED IN THE UNITED STATE OF AMERICA

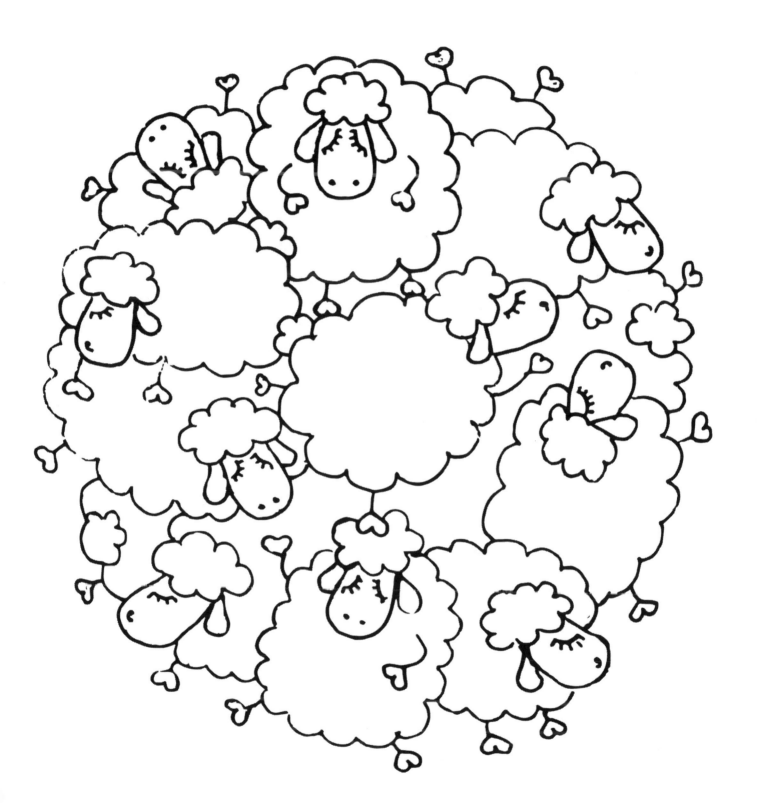

Printed in Poland
by Amazon Fulfillment
Poland Sp. z o.o., Wrocław